COMBAT WITHOUT WEAPONS

Capt. E. Hartley Leather, R.C.A.

PALADIN PRESS • BOULDER, COLORADO

Combat without Weapons
by Captain E. Hartley Leather, Royal Canadian Artillery

Original publication 1942; reprint by Paladin 2005

ISBN 13: 978-0-87364-060-2
Printed in the United States of America

Published by Paladin Press, a division of
Paladin Enterprises, Inc.
Gunbarrel Tech Center
7077 Winchester Circle
Boulder, Colorado 80301 USA
+1.303.443.7250

Direct inquiries and/or orders to the above address.

PALADIN, PALADIN PRESS, and the "horse head" design
are trademarks belonging to Paladin Enterprises and
registered in United States Patent and Trademark Office.

All rights reserved. Except for use in a review, no
portion of this book may be reproduced in any form
without the express written permission of the publisher.

Neither the author nor the publisher assumes
any responsibility for the use or misuse of
information contained in this book.

Visit our Web site at www.paladin-press.com

PREFACE

THIS little book was dedicated to the Home Guard, not generally but personally. To all the over-age, the under-age, the medically unfit, the sick, the lame and the blind. Its keynote is simplicity, and it is prepared solely for ordinary people, not for Commandos or professional wrestlers. Since "Combat Without Weapons" appeared I have been accused of being everything from just an ordinary thug to a downright sadist. I am neither: I have a real and genuine love for people and a very great love for living; I simply happen to believe that a knowledge of self-defence is a sound investment.

THE AUTHOR
CAPTAIN E. HARTLEY LEATHER
ROYAL CANADIAN ARTILLERY

IN 1942

H. V. MORTON wrote "In the Footsteps of the Master,"
"I Saw Two Englands," etc. etc.

THE Anti-Queensberry Rules set forth in this excellent booklet are inspired, so the author tells me, by the methods employed by the International Police Force at Shanghai. Their great virtue is that they are easily learnt and those who expound them need not be human gorillas.

I believe my Home Guard platoon was one of the first units of its kind to be instructed by Captain Leather, and I should like to say that we have derived great benefit from his teaching. Unarmed combat is a science which the author of these pages has studied with the utmost enthusiasm and has brought to a fine point of perfection by long practice. No one could say that it is a pleasant science; but then no one could say that this is a pleasant war. Captain Leather has skilfully put much of his teaching into these pages, and it can truthfully be said that every picture tells a story and every story thus told is of value to members of the Home Guard.

ACKNOWLEDGMENTS

MY sincere gratitude to all the members of my staff for their guidance and co-operation in preparing this pamphlet. In particular to Sergeant-Instructors J. D. Kane and E. A. Harsant, our pioneers of the gentle art, and E. Feist and G. A. Brabant, their very worthy successors, for the illustrations of this book and their hard and skilful work in demonstrating to Home Guards and County Police all over the South of England. Also to Messrs. Gale & Polden Ltd., my publishers, for their many helpful suggestions and for giving me this opportunity of putting this teaching before the public.

E. H. C. L.

ENGLAND.
December, 1942.

CONTENTS

	PAGE
INTRODUCTION	ix
RUTHLESSNESS	1
THE STEEL HELMET	3
VULNERABLE POINTS	5
THE KICK	6
OPPONENT UNARMED	7
WRIST RELEASE	9
HAIR OR CLOTHING HELD	9
STRANGLEHOLD	11
HELD AROUND THE WAIST	13
ARM LOCKS	13
ARM BREAK	17
OPPONENT ARMED	19
QUICK ACTION WITH A REVOLVER	23
PARRYING A RIFLE AND BAYONET	25
PARRYING A KNIFE	27
HOW TO USE A KNIFE	29
HOW TO USE A STICK	31
GROUND WORK	33
STALKING A SENTRY	35
TYING A PRISONER	37

INTRODUCTION

THIS little book is written with just two objects in view—brevity and simplicity. There are numerous texts on the subject, which is really a simplified version of the well-known judo. Unfortunately, most people still find it rather complicated and involved, and in this short volume we will try to reduce it to its lowest common denominator. Our idea is not to attempt to make specialists out of average people, but simply to teach a few simple tricks that everyone can learn in a matter of minutes, that will make you more efficient at self-defence.

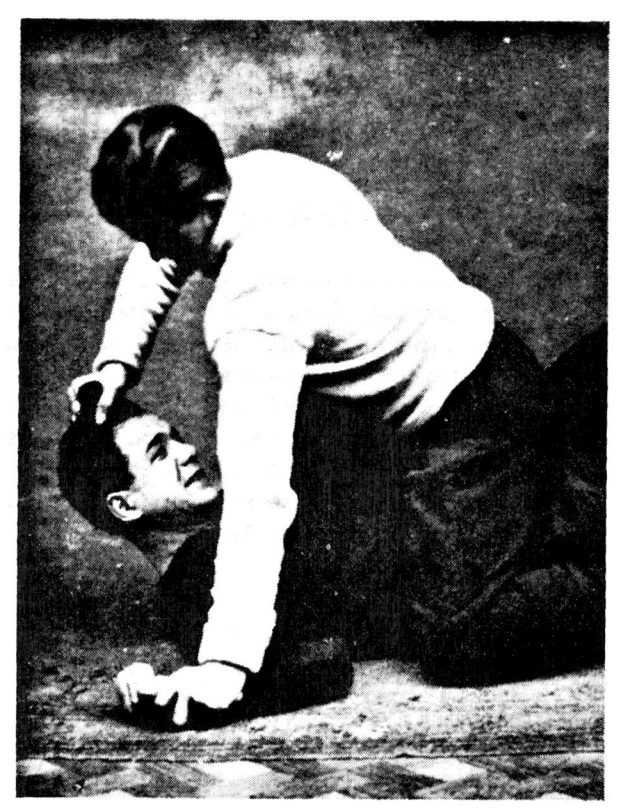

"SMASH HIS HEAD ON THE GROUND"

COMBAT WITHOUT WEAPONS

RUTHLESSNESS

Ruthlessness can best be defined in two words—speed and brutality. Your gentlemanly qualities will no doubt be offended by much of the following, but if you do not take it to heart it may be that at some future date your own neck will be a good deal more offended. In personal combat, as much as in the strategy of armies, the two chief elements of success are surprise and speed. It does not matter twopence what you do so long as you do it fast, and when you do it, do it as though your life depended on it, because it often does.

In my lectures I always maintained that the Home Guard should have a new motto, and my suggestion was **"Kick him in the crotch!"** That may at first sound just dirty, but in actual fact it happens to be the quickest, simplest and most foolproof way of dealing with any man, no matter how big and no matter how strong—**a knee in the right place may save your life.** In advancing for an attack nearly everyone except the expert leaves himself open well enough and long enough for you to do all that is necessary—that is the very minimum of action and risk on your part. Never waste energy; most of us have little enough to start with.

"START SWINGING IT"

"A GOOD BASH IN THE NOSE"

THE STEEL HELMET

The steel helmet was originally designed by some optimist as a protection against shell splinters and small-arms fire. Whether it is or not is rather a debatable point, but what most people do not realize is that it is a first-class weapon of offence, and in fact in really close work it is the last line of attack. One of the first principles of street fighting is **keep your man at arm's length,** where you can get at him and see what he is up to. But if he should get in close, grasp you around the waist, for instance, a good bash in the nose with the sharp edge of the helmet will soon make him let go. In order to make this even more effective, you might sharpen the edge of the rim with a file!

Many books illustrate some very effective releases from grips around the waist, under the arms; but after all no one but an absolute fool would ever grasp a man and leave both his arms free. If anyone does, he will get just what he deserves —a good right hook to the jaw. Do not confuse your mind with non-essentials—**get the fundamentals and get going!**

Assuming, then, that in all normal circumstances your opponent will first pin your arms to your side, what is your action? Presuming that he may well be stronger than you are, any arm or body movement on your part is sheer waste of energy. But you still have your head and your feet. If you are not wearing a helmet you should instinctively lash out with one or both feet; a badly bruised shin will keep its owner quite preoccupied

Do not think, however, that a bash on the face with the helmet is an end in itself; that only makes your opponent loosen up. Never half do a job. Once he has slackened off crack him in the jaw with your fist, or smash your knee into his crotch. Or, better, still, do both!

One last use for the "tin hat." If you are caught crowded in a confined space, your assailants not using firearms, just take it off and start swinging as you make for the door!

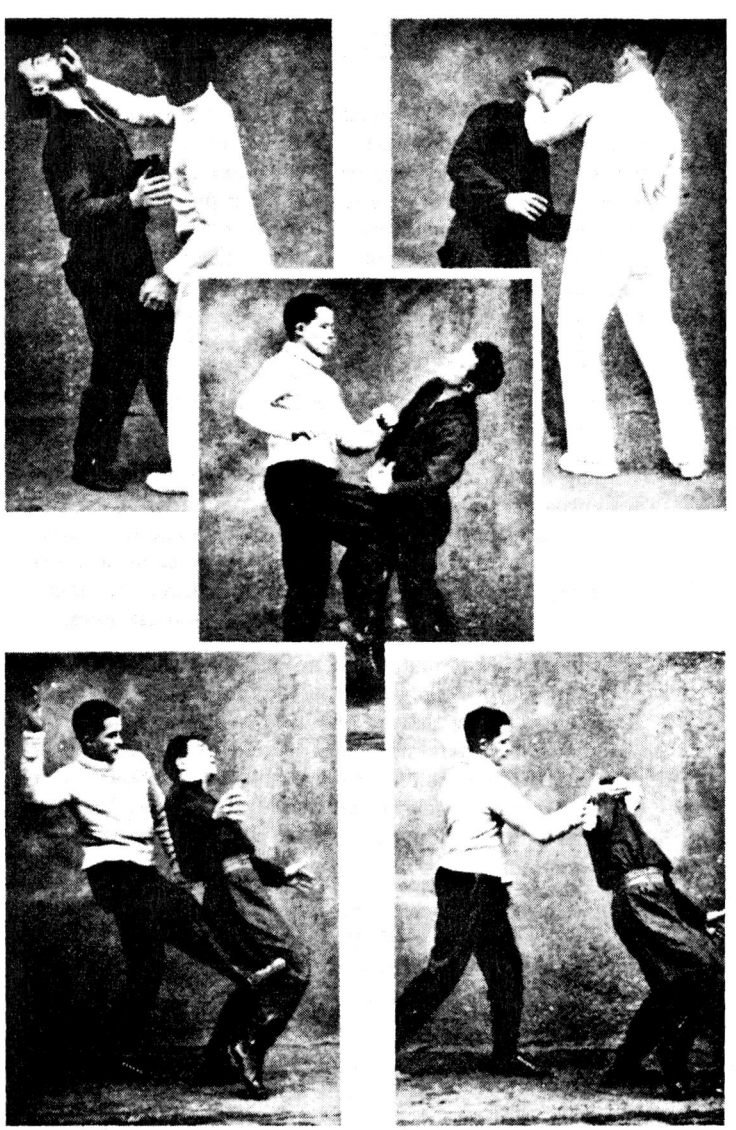

THE VULNERABLE POINTS ON A MAN'S BODY

VULNERABLE POINTS

A man's body is made up of many parts. Some are soft, some are hard. Some bend, some do not. In some places nerves are near the surface; in others they are not. Note these few points in the accompanying plates, and see how each may best be attacked.

Chin. If you are handy with your fists nothing can beat a good, solid punch on the jaw. A heel-of-the-hand punch also packs a terrific "wallop," and is much easier for those not experienced in the "gentle art."

Windpipe. A rabbit punch across the windpipe causes temporary black-out. While your man is in this dazed condition, finish him off—blow to the jaw, knee to the crotch, arm lock: what you will.

Sides of the Throat. A well-delivered punch just under the ears will at least dislocate the neck, and very probably break it.

Crotch. Probably the most vulnerable and sensitive part of the body. A knee or foot in the proper place from the weakest man will knock the strongest man senseless.

Kidneys and Small of Back. The main nerve and muscle cords of the body branch out like a tree from the base of the spine, and at this point are very near to the surface. A two-fisted punch here has a great stunning effect. If delivered quickly a man cannot even cry out.

Knees. When stalking a man from behind, a kick in the back of the knee will make him "fold up," and give you a much better target for finishing the job efficiently.

Arms. There are three joints in the arm—the wrist, elbow and shoulder. They are all designed to bend one way and one way only. If you force them the other way they must either break or your man goes down. The choice is up to him, and it is immaterial to you.

Also, note from these plates that there are three good ways of punching—the fist, the rabbit punch, and the heel-of-the-hand punch. The last two, although not so widely known, are very effective. A heel of the hand in the jaw snaps the head back and may very easily break the neck. A rabbit punch on the soft part of the neck or base of the skull may be equally disconcerting for your opponent, and do just as much damage. Their beauty is in their simplicity. A man not used to using his fists may very easily dislocate a finger or break a thumb if he is not very careful.

THE KICK

An ordinary straight kick is a narrow object aimed at a narrow target, and the slightest move on your opponent's part may cause you to miss, leaving you wide open for his attentions. Kick him with the inside of the foot and aim at a point about a foot behind his instep. Make contact a few inches below the knee and scrape downwards, putting all the weight into the finish across his ankle joint. This has the effect of scraping all the skin off his shin and smashing all the small bones on the top of his foot, a very tender and unprotected part of the body. It renders the foot completely useless, and as your man topples forward finish him with an uppercut to the jaw or the knee in the crotch.

Always remember that a kick on the shins will make the strongest man lurch forward and bend in the middle—in other words, stick his chin out. Chins in this position were meant for uppercuts. If you are not sure of your punch, pull him forwards and downwards by the neck or shoulders and bring your knee up to meet his face as it comes down!

And once again remember the vital questions of energy and risk. Never take unnecessary chances; your man may be down, but that does not say he is out. Don't muck about with him! Heads on the ground call for the same treatment as footballs—put the boots to him! He probably deserves it.

OPPONENT UNARMED

There is an old saying that the burglar is usually more nervous than the burgled: after all, he probably doesn't know his way around your house as well as you do, to take only one example. In dealing with any kind of attack the best defence is usually the quickest, and vice versa.

Personally, I always like to keep a saying of the great Lord Nelson's in mind: "*I am convinced that the boldest action is always the safest.*"

First let us recognize that whether a man comes at you or you go at him, the first things you are going to make contact with are his arms. Nobody starts a fight with his hands behind his back. Therefore there are only two cases worth consideration—either he grips you first or you grip him.

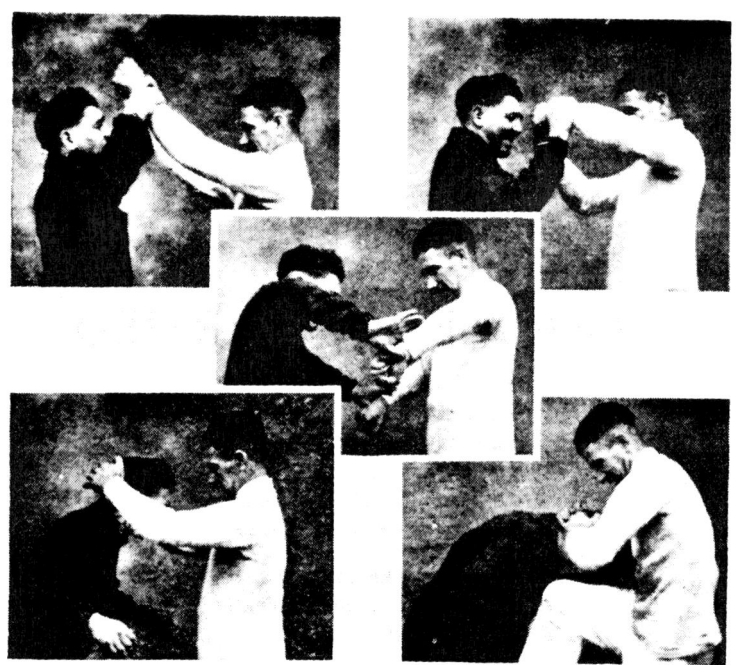

WRIST RELEASE

CLOTHING HELD

WRIST RELEASE

His first grasp will invariably be at your wrists or forearms. Look at the plate. He will have four fingers on one side of your arm and only his thumb on the other side. Work on the thumb. The strongest man's thumb will not be stronger than your whole arm. To achieve the maximum force and surprise, start by lifting your arms upwards; then as your man exerts force to pull them down again swing them down and out, pressing against his thumb. He will have to let go: it is impossible to hold on. By swinging down and out vigorously your arms will come free above his and his body will be jerked forward. Continue your arm swing to the back of his head and bring the knee upwards, thus smashing his face on your kneecap, stepping slightly forward as you do to ensure a large surface of contact and the maximum damage.

HAIR OR CLOTHING HELD

You will readily see from the plate that to grasp a person in this manner means a right-angular bend in the wrist to start with. In other words, a maximum bend. Bend it any more and he must either bend his whole body or let go. If done with speed he will almost invariably let go, and the chances of breaking his wrist are equally good. Hold your hands straight and rigid together, using the sharp edge to press into his wrist joint; step in close and bend forward from the shoulders, at the same time giving him your knee in the crotch. This will get you free and leave you in a position for a blow to the jaw, or smash his face against your knee. This release is correct when grasped with one or both hands, and any place between the shoulders and the waist.

RELEASE FROM STRANGLEHOLD

STRANGLEHOLD

Whether from the front or behind, and get this straight, *it is physically impossible for you to be throttled provided you keep your head;* and it is easy to keep your head if you will realize how small is your actual danger, no man with courage or knowledge would ever use a stranglehold. It is—or should be, provided you "know your stuff"—suicide.

In actual fact, this may be very easily tested by the weakest woman. In the first place, in order to strangle you the great majority of people will put themselves in a position where the well-known sensitive spot is well within range—use your knee! Being purely defensive, if you pull your chin well in, there is very little left for anyone to strangle. Further, in order to strangle you your assailant must leave his fingers in a place well within your reach. Get the little one and jerk it back; his hand then must come clear of your throat. Don't take my word for it: try it and see for yourself. When you're satisfied, and therefore confident, *try* the next step.

Grasp your opponent's opposite wrists—that is, cross your hands, taking his right in yours, and his left in yours, right arm under, left arm over as shown in the plate. Push out on both his arms. This will make him force inward, which is just what you want him to do. When you feel this extra pressure, twist your body slightly to the left, pulling your own arms apart, thus crossing your opponent's arms above the elbow. Hold his left hand close to your body, bending his right arm across it. This will force your opponent off balance to his left rear. As he is falling give him your right knee in the crotch.

It may well be pointed out that I have only considered the ordinary Western or hand strangles, and disregarded judo methods altogether. This is perfectly true, but judo experts, like myself, must remember that they are in a very small minority; strangulation with the hands is much the most common form in Western countries, but even when gripped between a person's arms the same principles apply—keep calm, use your feet or knees if at all possible, and go for his crotch. I have found the results quite satisfactory.

THE FLYING MARE

HELD AROUND THE WAIST

As already stated, the first principle of this kind of rough-and-tumble is to keep your opponent at arm's length. The idea is simply that you want to inflict as much damage with as little done to yourself as possible. The second and only other rule to remember is **never go to the ground with your opponent**. It is obvious that this means getting close to him, and once again being close you will not have room to see what he is up to or to work yourself.

However, if you are so unfortunate as to get caught around the waist, particularly from behind, there is no need to give up the ghost. There is also no need to wriggle and struggle and try to get your arms free simply by pushing and shoving. Remember, energy is precious: do not waste it. You have already been shown how to use a helmet in such an emergency. Obviously with both arms pinned to your sides, the only other weapons you have to work with are your feet. The moment you feel yourself grasped in this manner lash out for his shins, and/or give him your knee in his crotch: he is very vulnerable to both these forms of attack, and does not know his job or he would not have attacked you in this fashion. This will make him loosen his grip and give you a chance to get your arms free, whereupon you can apply a punch or an arm lock—as shown elsewhere in this pamphlet.

ARM LOCKS

In first analysing fighting we reduced it to two categories only; we have shown you how to handle a man who tries to wrestle with you; now let us consider the fighter who wants to use his fists. Take my advice and don't use your own unless you really know how; the art of boxing takes skill and practice, and the result of faulty punches is invariably damaged hands and fingers.

The first and most obvious place any man will try to strike you is in the face. With which hand is immaterial, though the right is far the most common for obvious reasons. If the blow

THE ELBOW BREAK

ARM LOCKS—continued

is aimed for your face the answer is the flying mare; if it comes low at your stomach then the elbow break. In answering the "that's all right for an expert but I could never do that" school, let me point out a few very simple facts. Visualize yourself driving along a road at thirty miles an hour. A child suddenly rushes into your path three yards in front of your car. What chance have you got of *not* hitting that child? Perhaps you may well know from bitter experience. Now transpose the analogy. The car is your assailant's fist, the driver himself, and you are the child. This time you are the target the blow is trying to hit. Now, if at a range of three feet or even less you suddenly move even a few inches, what are his chances of redirecting his aim to hit you in your new position? Exactly the same as before—extremely small. Deflection, after all, is one of the first essentials of boxing. If it were not, every blow would end in a knock-out. An exaggerated movement is not necessary; pivoting on your forward foot will shift your head by six inches, which is quite sufficient. Now, assuming that you are convinced, here are the details.

THE FLYING MARE

First, the flying mare. Grasp your opponent's right wrist or forearm with both hands. Pivot quickly on the left foot, carrying his arm over your own left shoulder, so that your shoulder comes between his elbow and his shoulder, twisting his wrist to keep the palm of his hand uppermost—this is most important, otherwise he will be able to bend his elbow and the break will not work. It will readily be seen that the slightest downward pressure in this position will cause his arm to break, using your own shoulder as the fulcrum.

THE ELBOW BREAK

Next, the elbow break, which is also of use as a "come along," as a man can be kept under control without any discomfort or danger to yourself. In this you grasp your oppo-

THE ARM BREAK

nent's right wrist or forearm in your own right, pivot on the right foot, swinging the left to a position just beside your opponent's right foot. At the same time, throw your left arm over above his elbow, and under it again to bring your left hand across your own body. Now by applying a downward pressure to his arm with your right hand his elbow can easily be broken across your own left arm, which is braced across your own body. To make your grip firmer, grasp your own right arm with your left hand as you are holding him.

ARM BREAK

This is simply a fast method of elbow breaking, for use when your man comes at you on the run. Remembering the element of surprise, make use of his own speed to bring about his downfall. As he advances stand your ground firmly. As he sets himself to charge you he unconsciously judges his distance and the exact spot where he expects to make contact. By waiting till the last possible moment and then moving slightly to the side, you throw his calculations just a few inches off and he is for an instant off balance and coming forward with a fair degree of speed. In this case we will assume that you made a turn half-left, pivoting quickly on the right foot. As he reaches you, arms outstretched to grasp or strike you, seize his right arm with both hands. Jerk his arm forward to increase his speed, and as he goes past you throw your left shoulder vigorously into his arm behind his shoulder and his elbow.

"ALWAYS THE BOLDEST ACTION"

OPPONENT ARMED

It must be obvious to everyone that if you have no weapon and your opponent has one you are in a pretty sticky position. However, let me suggest this to you. He is attacking, he is armed, you are not, his business is to harm you; either you sit back and "take it," or you put up a fight for your life. Personally, I prefer to fight; and if you have any Irish in you you will prefer to fight anyway. This brings us back to the first principle of military strategy—the element of surprise. If he is armed and you are not, the last thing he expects is that you will attack him. Therefore half your object is achieved from the start: it is only necessary once again to execute your movement with speed and vigour. Remember Lord Nelson—"always the boldest action."

You will remember that when both of you are unarmed we told you to keep your man at arm's length; when he is armed the opposite applies. The reason for this is simple enough. If you crowd him he will not have room to use his weapon, whatever it is, and also you will have a better chance of getting your hands on it when you can.

First we will consider close quarters against a man with a tommy-gun, automatic pistol or revolver. If he shoots you before you can get close to him—well, that is "one on the house," and the more fool you for not stalking him carefully. However, we are considering that you can get close to him without committing suicide. The most effective action is to half-turn the body, quickly crashing the forearm, on the appropriate side, against his weapon as near as possible to his hand. A really good blow with a hard, bony arm will usually knock the weapon completely out of his hand, and even if it does not you have decreased the size of the target and forced the gun off your own body. As you will see from the plate, it is now pointing past you and not at you, and therefore there is no immediate danger. From here apply either an arm lock or hit him on the jaw, or kick him in the place where it hurts most.

"IF HE DIGS HIS GUN IN YOUR BACK"

Next we will take the case where you are being taken prisoner—a most futile pastime at best; that is where your assailant has his weapon, tommy-gun or revolver, either in your back or in your stomach. First a few simple points in handling this type of weapon. Let me tell you a short story of an incident a few years ago in Chicago. A policeman was detailed to make an arrest. When he walked into the culprit's office the man snatched up a revolver and pointed it at the policeman's head. The latter walked calmly across the room, disarmed his man and arrested him. He was hailed as a hero. As he pointed out himself, he was never in any danger at all. Why? It is simple. In the first place, no one who knows how to use a revolver ever points it at your head; because all revolvers "jump," and the shot would have gone completely over his head, even if it had been fired. Secondly, if your man intends to shoot you he will do so at once and not give you the opportunity to turn the tables on him. In the same way, if a man digs his gun in your back or stomach, he obviously does not intend to shoot you—not at once, at any rate. One-tenth of a second is all you need in which to act. Look at the plate: from back or front the action is the same. When he makes you raise your hands never put them up straight; hold them as far apart as possible, then he cannot focus both arms at the same time. Once again sweep the arm down and strike his hand where he grips the weapon, half turning the body as you do so. His gun will now be pointing off your body and you will have him off guard. By this time you should know what to do next.

Practise this with an empty revolver and tell your opponent to really try to pull the trigger. The author has made it a point in all his demonstrations to ask people to come up and try to shoot him; he can honestly say that no one has ever succeeded. It takes far longer for him to "get wise" to what you are up to and to make up his mind to press the trigger than it does for you to make that simple movement with your arm; literally, this never fails. Try it with an empty gun and you will soon be convinced of the truth.

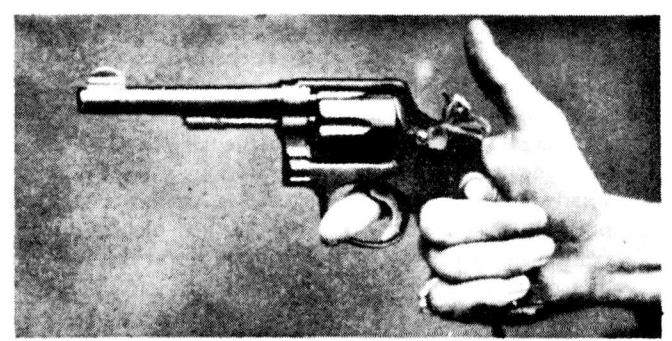
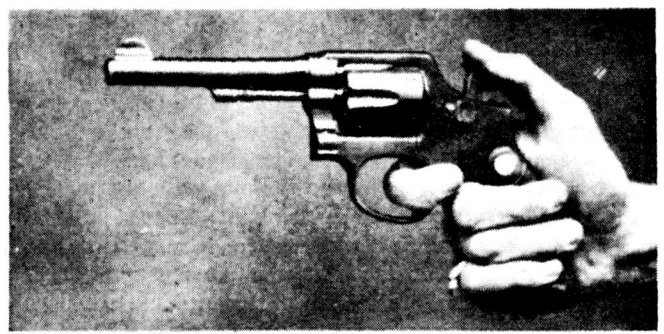
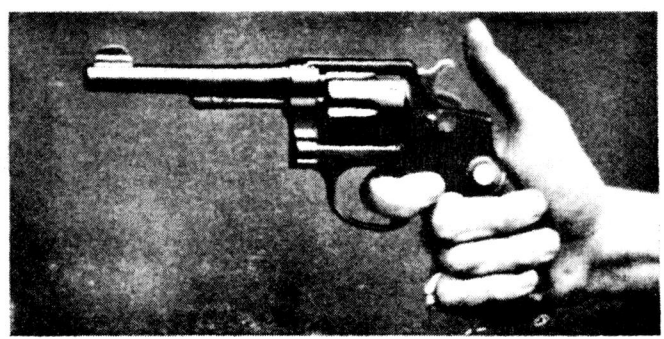

A SPLIT SECOND—ONE MAN DIES

QUICK ACTION WITH A REVOLVER

Now here is just one trick which you may not know which could actually give the lie to what I have just written. The reason I have felt safe in writing as I did is because I have never met one man, except the one who taught me, who knew this trick, and therefore I assume that it is more or less unknown amongst the general public. It is absolutely the quickest and most foolproof way of using a revolver, but unfortunately cannot be done with an automatic.

Assume any case where you know that you are going to have to shoot, and shoot fast; reconnoitring buildings or any areas where the enemy are believed to be present, stalking a man, especially in the dark. Remembering our analogy of the man driving a car, just figure out the situation. First you encounter your opponent. Your nervous reaction tells your brain that the time has come to pull the trigger. You take an appreciable time, long enough not to get killed, to decide on your action and telegraph the impulse to your trigger finger and actually pull the trigger. Even when the revolver is cocked this will take a definite time—time in which you may die.

The trick is simplicity itself. It makes firing instantaneous and dependent on that first nervous reaction alone. It practically eliminates jumping. Cock the revolver, put your thumb firmly on the cocking handle and pull the trigger. Then the pressure of your thumb alone is preventing the gun from going off, and the slightest reaction on your part, that natural psychological "jump" which always happens when your target actually comes into sight, will cause the thumb to release the cocking handle and the gun goes off by itself.

PARRYING A RIFLE AND BAYONET

PARRYING A RIFLE AND BAYONET

A bayonet is probably the toughest proposition a man can be asked to face. But, once again, you have only this simple choice: either you let Nature take its course and hope the insurance company will take care of your family or you fight for it. He obviously intends to kill you, anyway, so you might as well go down fighting; and if you learn this easy trick properly your chances of survival are remarkably good. The secret of the whole thing is that you must stand your ground to the very last possible moment, and move only when your opponent is right on top of you. That takes guts, true, but if you don't the opponent will take a good deal more.

As your opponent comes at you, parry the rifle to your left with your left forearm, and grasp his leading hand firmly with your left hand. Pivot the body half-left from the left foot, and seize his left arm just below the shoulder. Hold with the left hand and press down with the right; as your man bends kick him violently with your right knee on his rear end. He must either go down or drop his rifle. This leaves him bent double with his back to you and you holding the rifle; transfer the right hand to the rifle and smash the butt into his head.

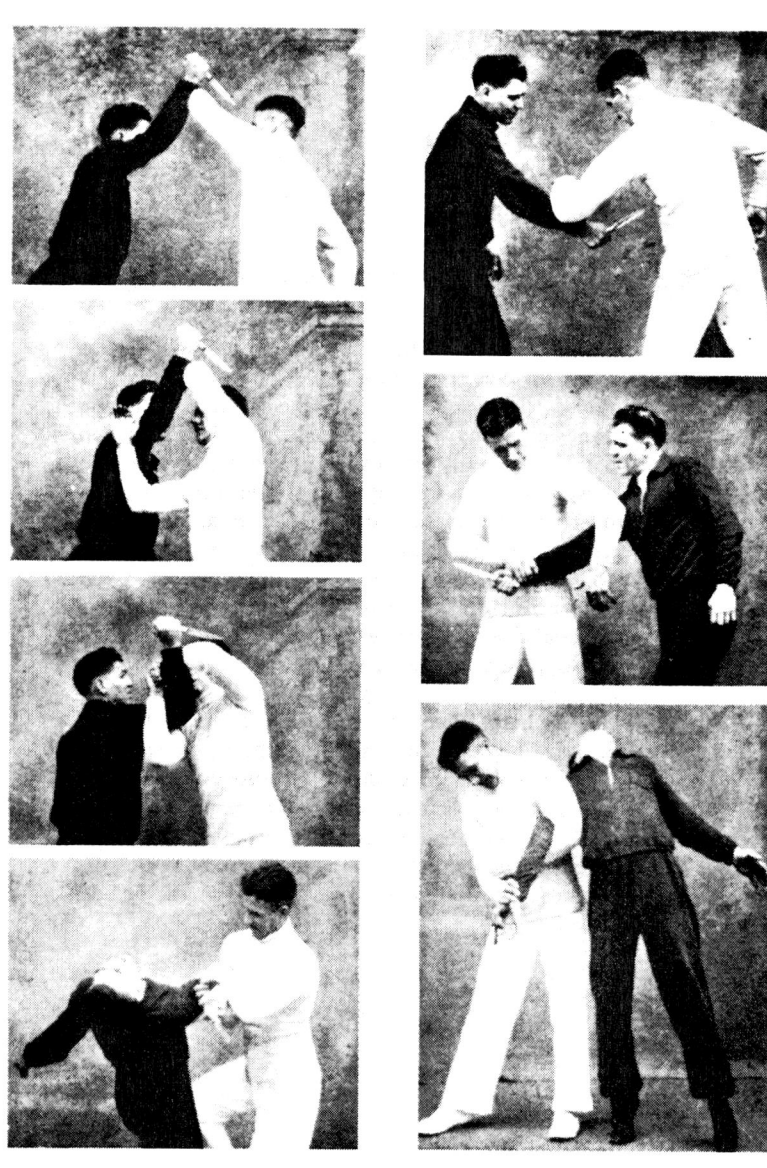

PARRYING A KNIFE

PARRYING A KNIFE

It is not perhaps generally realized how many unpleasant characters carry knives, and know how to use them. Once again you are undoubtedly in a spot; and the only successful action must be taken from a firm stand: if you raise your arm to parry the blow while your opponent is still ten feet away from you, it will be an easy matter for him to change his direction and foil you. You must wait till the last possible moment before you act. As he comes to strike, raise your left forearm horizontally across your face, catching his forearm across yours. Swing the right arm under his right between his elbow and his shoulder. Clasp your hands together and press to his right rear—that is your left front—at the same time giving him your right knee in the crotch. This is another version of the elbow break, and he must go down; you have your whole weight and both arms concentrated against his right forearm.

The action is very similar for the odd case in which your assailant uses an understroke rather than an overstroke. The forearm parry is exactly the same except that you parry low rather than high, as shown in the plate. From here an arm lock can be very simply applied with the desired results.

Both these methods are equally effective against an opponent who swings at you with a side sweep; if his arm is in the top half of a semi-circle use the first; if the bottom half the second method shown.

THE SHORT ROUTE TO THE STOMACH

HOW TO USE A KNIFE

Now that does not by any means preclude the use of knives: after all, every little bit helps, and a good sharp knife properly handled can make you a dangerous man exactly to the same degree that one badly handled is perfectly useless.

If you have some favourite method of your own by all means use it. I am simply going to show you the action I have found to be most simple and effective, in the hope that it may be of help. I carry my knife in a holster strapped just inside my right-hand pocket, where it is out of sight but available with the touch of the fingertips. With a little practice at drawing you will rapidly find that this defence is practically unbeatable. Stand your ground as your man comes at you; wait till the last possible moment. If he is armed, parry the blow with your left arm and let him run himself on to your knife, which is whipped out just in time with your right and simply braced against your hip.

If you are attacking, exactly the same thing applies. Don't show him your knife first, even if he is armed to the teeth; keep the pleasant surprises to the last. And once again the minimum of action; when you draw from the hip his stomach is the nearest and easiest target and therefore the right one.

One last word about striking from behind. Never take a chance of plunging a knife into a man's back : he might have a thick coat, a leather belt. There is just a chance of a slip-up. Don't take it. Use his neck : there is hardly any known article of clothing or protective plate which covers that, and it is always within reach. If you are small, strike upwards and aim for the ear on the opposite side. If you are tall, strike down between the backbone and collarbone.

"RAM THE STICK IN HIS STOMACH"

HOW TO USE A STICK

One of the most innocent of weapons is an ordinary stick, such as officers usually carry, or any bit of wood of comparable size and shape. Innocent but because of that very fact extremely effective. If anyone attacks you while you are holding such a weapon he may not notice it at all, or if he does it is most probable that he will expect you to swing at him with it, which is actually what most people try to do. This is ineffective because the swing, like a hay-maker, is usually wild and can be easily parried or ducked away from.

Use the stick just like a knife. If he runs at you ram the stick forward so that he takes it in the stomach, or if his arms are not directly in the way jab him in the throat. I know it's not nice, but you may not look very pleasant with your throat slit either.

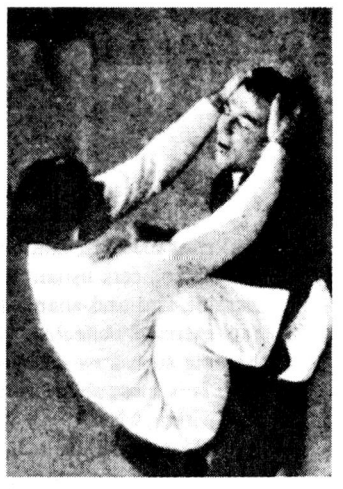

"DON'T WASTE TIME OR ENERGY ON THE GROUND"

GROUND WORK

You have already been told never to go to the ground with a man; however, accidents happen in the best-regulated families, so it may even happen that you are attacked while you are sleeping, or otherwise lying on the ground. Here again there are only two alternatives worth considering. Your man will either try to throttle you or hit you in the face. In either case, his arms will be in front of your face and easily reached for an arm lock, which, combined with a twist of the body, will reverse your positions. The arm lock is applied exactly as for the stranglehold in the standing position. He will obviously have both arms in the fray, and therefore you have two arms to work on.

As you cross his arms as already taught, vigorously twist the body and throw upwards with your hips. This will throw the man off you, and the twisting of his arms will put you on top. As mentioned in the beginning, when you have a man in this position do not waste time and energy in either of the futile pursuits of hitting or strangling. Grab his hair, his ears or just his head in general, and smash it recklessly on the ground.

"GET HIM UNDER CONTROL WITHOUT A SOUND"

STALKING A SENTRY

There are many versions of this, but I have chosen the one which I believe can be carried out with the least amount of physical exertion and the greatest degree of safety. There are, I think, one or two more effective ways of getting your man under control speedily, but they all call for a considerable degree of strength and skill, and therefore I shall not recommend them here.

In stalking a man from behind, your object is to get him under control without a sound; and that means preventing him from crying out when he is seized. Careful stalking to get yourself in a position to strike is, of course, a first essential, but that in itself is outside our present scope. In order to silence your man at the first contact, the initial blow must be at his throat, and I trust by now that you will know enough not to try throttling him with your hands.

At this point we make a gracious bow in the direction of the judo experts. Swing the left arm across his throat, keeping it perfectly rigid, fingers tensed, thumb kept close to the palm. That gives you a sharp rather than a rounded edge next to his throat and is more painful. Next bring the right arm up to the back of his neck, securing your left hand in your own right elbow joint. Once again keep the hand extended with the sharp edge of the forearm against his neck. It will now be seen that his neck is secured firmly between your two arms and you have perfect leverage to apply the pressure. One word of caution—when applying this hold try to keep your own body turned so far as possible away from your victim so that your legs and crotch are out of harm's way.

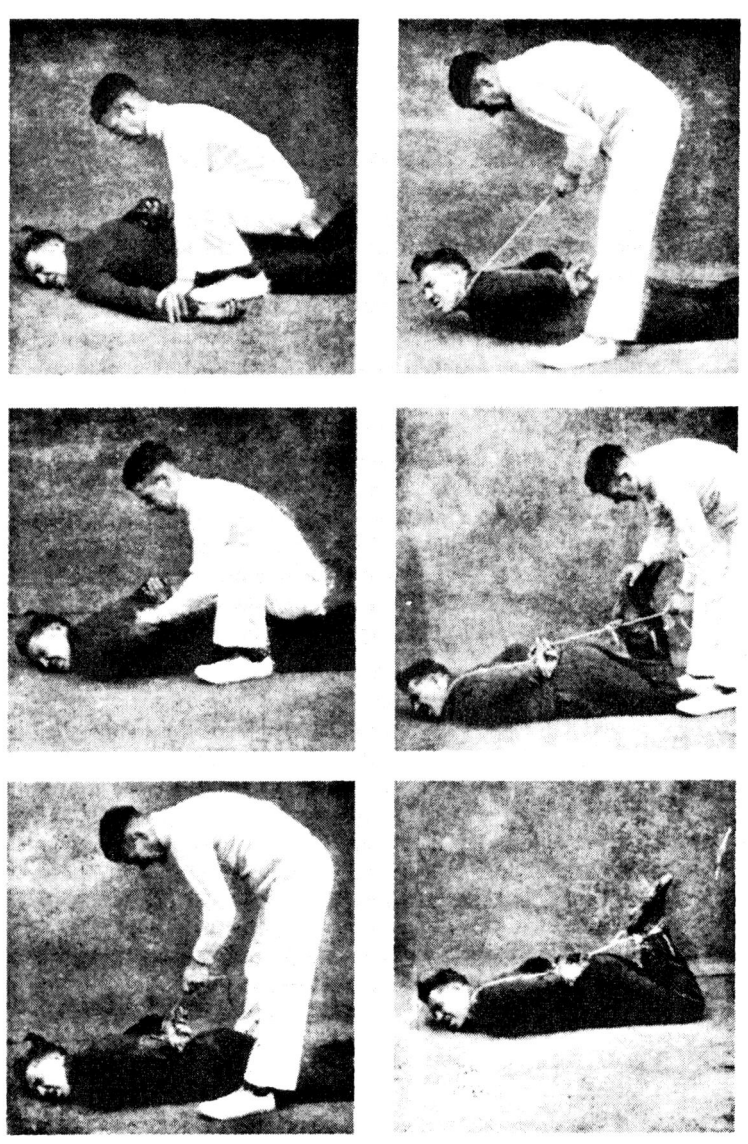

"THERE IS NO POSSIBLE WAY OUT OF THIS"